DUCKS

by Meg Gaertner

Cody Koala

An Imprint of Pop!
popbooksonline.com

abdobooks.com

Published by Pop!, a division of ABDO, PO Box 398166, Minneapolis, Minnesota 55439. Copyright © 2019 by POP, LLC. International copyrights reserved in all countries. No part of this book may be reproduced in any form without written permission from the publisher. Pop!™ is a trademark and logo of POP, LLC.

Printed in the United States of America, North Mankato, Minnesota.

092018
012019

THIS BOOK CONTAINS RECYCLED MATERIALS

Cover Photo: iStockphoto
Interior Photos: iStockphoto, 1, 5 (top), 15 (bottom left); Shutterstock Images, 5 (bottom left), 5 (bottom right), 6, 9, 10, 11, 13, 15 (top), 15 (bottom right), 16, 19, 21

Editor: Charly Haley
Series Designer: Laura Mitchell

Library of Congress Control Number: 2018950116

Publisher's Cataloging-in-Publication Data

Names: Gaertner, Meg, author.
Title: Ducks / by Meg Gaertner.
Description: Minneapolis, Minnesota: Pop!, 2019 | Series: Pond animals | Includes online resources and index.
Identifiers: ISBN 9781532162077 (lib. bdg.) | ISBN 9781641855785 (pbk) | ISBN 9781532163135 (ebook)
Subjects: LCSH: Ducks--Juvenile literature. | Ducks--Behavior--Juvenile literature. | Pond animals--Juvenile literature.
Classification: DDC 598.410--dc23

Hello! My name is

Cody Koala

Pop open this book and you'll find QR codes like this one, loaded with information, so you can learn even more!

Scan this code* and others like it while you read, or visit the website below to make this book pop.

popbooksonline.com/ducks

*Scanning QR codes requires a web-enabled smart device with a QR code reader app and a camera.

Table of Contents

Chapter 1

Water Bird

Ducks are birds that spend a lot of time in water. They live in ponds, lakes, and rivers. They can be found worldwide.

Watch a video here!

wings for flying

flat bill

feathers

webbed feet for swimming

Ducks have flat **bills** and webbed feet. Their feet help them swim. Special oil on their feathers keeps them from getting wet.

Chapter 2

Swimming Along

Ducks swim, walk, and fly. They eat plants, seeds, and insects in the water and near the shore.

Learn more here!

Some ducks lift their tails in the air. They duck their heads underwater to find food. Other ducks dive deep for food.

Ducks keep themselves clean by **preening**. They run their bills over their feathers.

They remove dust and dirt.
They spread oil over their
feathers to stay dry.

Ducks lose their feathers and then grow new ones. This is called **molting**.

The Life of a Duck

Male ducks have brightly colored feathers to attract **females**. Ducks pair up in the winter. Then the female chooses a place to lay her eggs in the spring.

Learn more here!

The female builds a nest of leaves, grass, and soft feathers. She lays six to 12 eggs. She sits on them for almost a month to keep them warm. The eggs hatch, and baby ducks are born.

The female raises the baby ducks. She protects them. Baby ducks can fly in a few weeks. They are ready to have their own babies within a year.

Ducks live five to ten years in the wild.

Chapter 4

Migration

Ducks do not live in one place all year. They **migrate** south for the winter. Many ducks fly together.

Only female ducks quack.

Complete an activity here!

Making Connections

Text-to-Self

Have you ever seen a duck? If not, have you seen another animal in the wild?

Text-to-Text

Have you read another book about a different animal? How is that animal similar to a duck? How is it different?

Text-to-World

Ducks spend time in water and on land. Can you think of any other animals that spend time on both water and land?

Glossary

bill – a bird's beak.

female – a person or animal of the sex that can have babies or lay eggs.

male – a person or animal of the sex that cannot have babies or lay eggs.

migrate – to move from one place to another when the seasons change.

molt – to shed old feathers for new ones.

preen – for a bird to clean and smooth its feathers with its beak.

Index

Online Resources

popbooksonline.com

Thanks for reading this Cody Koala book!

Scan this code* and others like it in this book, or visit the website below to make this book pop!

popbooksonline.com/ducks

*Scanning QR codes requires a web-enabled smart device with a QR code reader app and a camera.